PICCOLO & ADAMS RECIPES

Italian Family Home Cooking

Italian recipes passed down from Nonna Piccolo and the children of the family Adams

At last, here it is! Genuine Napoli style recipes handed down by Mum (aka: Nonna). Not like what you find in Italian restaurants. Lasagne stuffed full of what's available and definitely no bechamel sauce. Fried pizza with a unique olive – caper sauce. Garlic and prezzemolo in the plenty. Move over, Jamie, your time is up.

This is the REAL stuff.

Copyright © 2024

Christopher James Adams

All Rights Reserved.

ISBN: 9798879914979

Introduction 4

NONNA'S RECIPES

Napoli Style Pizza 6
Meat Tomato Sauce 8
Potato Pie 10
Roasted Potatoes in Garlic 12
Minestrone 14
Brodo (Vegetable Broth With Soup Pasta) 16
Schnitzels 18
Bean Soup 20
Fried Green Leaves 22
Rice Balls 24
Spicy Tomato Sauce 26
Meat Balls 28
Gnocchi 30
Peas with Onions 32
Roast Fish Fillets 34
Roast Pork Chops 36
Potatoes in Tomatoes and Garlic 38
Courgette / Aubergine (Eggplant) In Egg Batter 40
Pork Onion Pepper Sauce For Pasta 42
Tender Fried Peppers 44
Fried Left Over Spaghetti Bolognese 46
Garlic Toast 48
Napoli Style Lasagne 50
Chicken Diavolo 52

CHRIS'S RECIPES

Classic Tomato Sauce 54
Authentic Ragù / Bolognese Sauce With Pasta 56
Basil Pesto 58
Pesto Pasta 60
Caprese Salad 62
Carbonara 64
Lentils Pasta 66
Kale & Olives Pasta 68
Creamy Mushroom Pasta 70
Creamy Broccoli Pasta 72
Italian Style Picked Eggs 74
Kale and Salami Omelette 76
Marinated Olives 78
Tips **80**

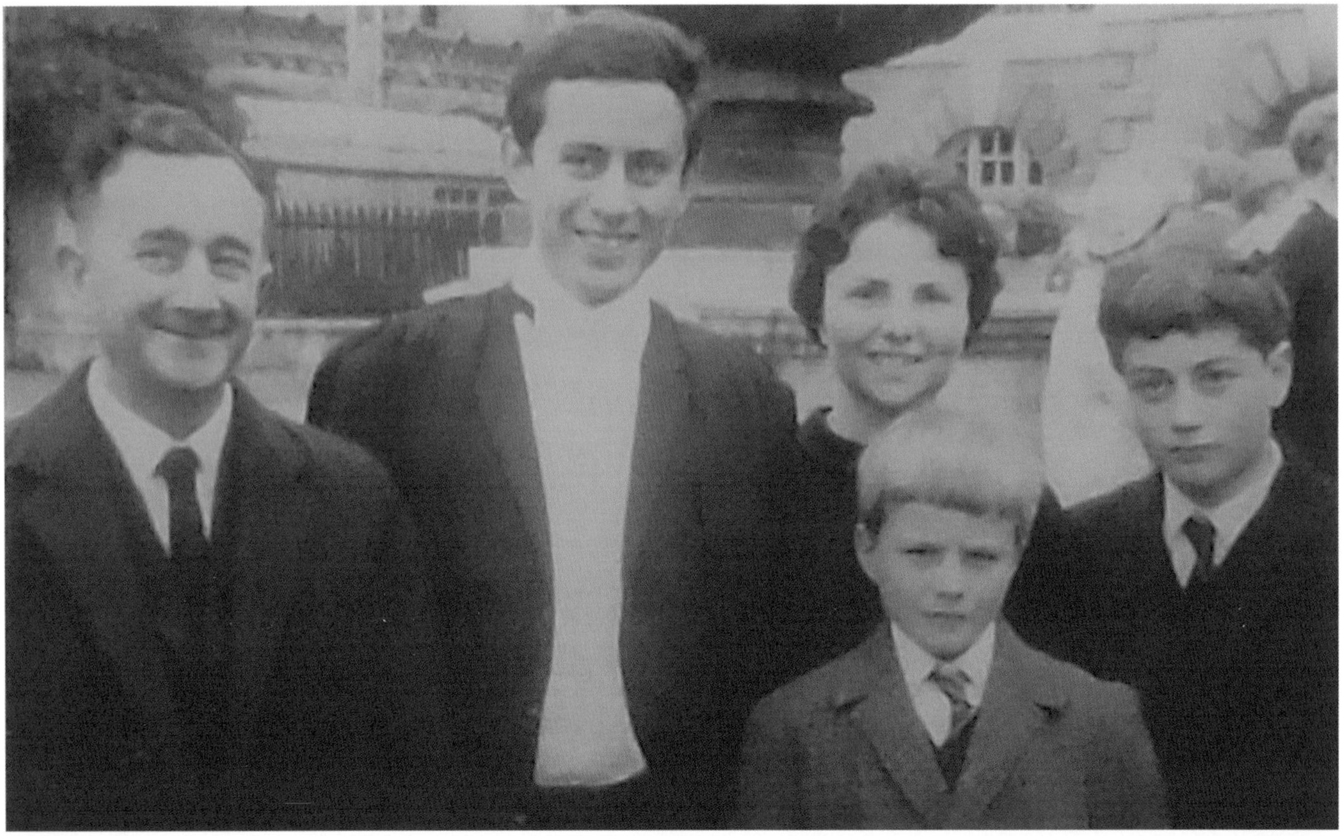

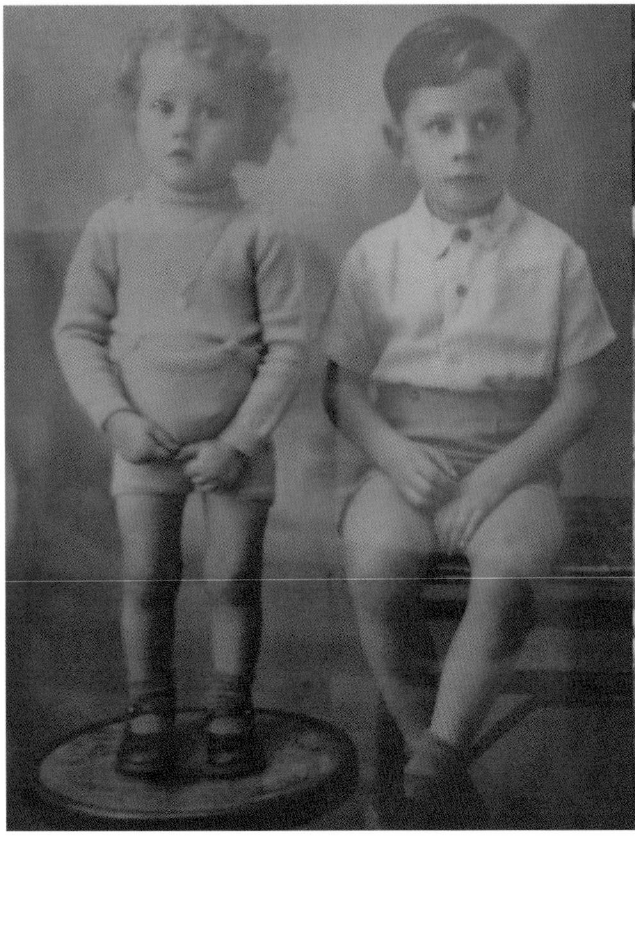

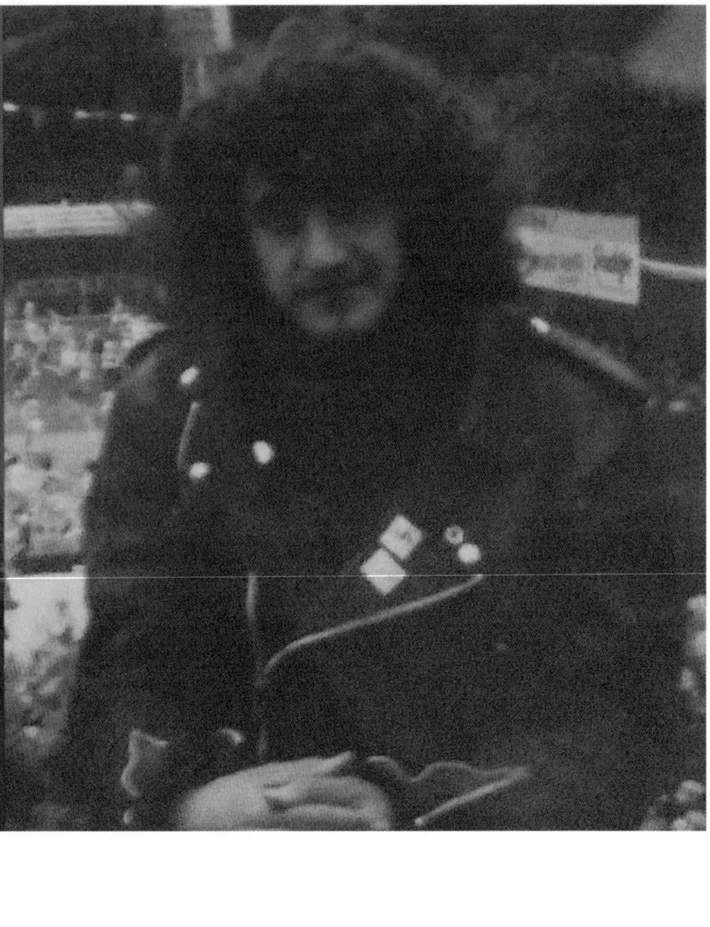

Many, many years before Jamie, the Adams - Piccolo family (William, Ron, Eric and Frank) already knew about crushed garlic, alla dente, parsley, olive oil and fried spaghetti. It was all taken for granted in our 1960s and spaghetti was certainly not from tins as our British childhood contemporaries thought. Tomato sauce was cooked for hours using fresh ingredients, not squeezed out of a bottle. Pizzas were fried. Lasagna was stuffed full with whatever was available.

Our mother, now known as Nonna because of the next generation (Chris, Nick) hailed from Napoli. A normal discussion sounded like an argument. An argument was hysteria. Amongst this colourful childhood was the cooking. Real Napoli style. Even to this day, I have not found genuine lasagne, pizza and potato pie in Italian restaurants. Nor rice balls or brodo. Jamie has made an admirable effort, but has missed a few.

So here, thanks to Chris who put this manuscript together, are my mother's (aka Nonna) genuine Napoli recipes together with a few modified versions by Chris and Nick, commensurate with modern day trends. Enjoy!

Eric Adams

NAPOLI STYLE PIZZA

Approx total time: 1hr 30min

INGREDIENTS (PIZZA DOUGH)

- 3 Cups (300ml Cup) Bread Flour
- 2 Tablespoons Extra Virgin Olive Oil
- 2 Teaspoons Salt
- 2 Teaspoons Dried Yeast
- 1 Tablespoon Sugar
- About 240 Ml Water

METHOD (PIZZA DOUGH)

1. Mix all ingredients together with enough water to give a sticky but firm dough.

2. Knead well for 10 minutes, add to a bowl and cover the bowl with a warm, damp tea-cloth.

3. Leave to rise in a warm place for about 40 minutes to 1 hour.

INGREDIENTS (PIZZA SAUCE)

- Half Onion
- 2 Cloves Garlic
- 80 Grams Black Olives, Sliced In Two
- 1/2 Handful Of Salted Capers
- 1 Can Peeled Plum Tomatoes
- 2 Tablespoons Tomato Puree
- Tablespoon Fresh Chapped Parsley
- Good Handful Of Dried Oregano
- Extra Virgin Olive Oil

METHOD (PIZZA SAUCE)

1. Slice the onions and garlic and fry gently in a saucepan in olive oil until soft. Do not allow to brown.

2. Add the tomatoes and puree, olives, parsley and capers. Simmer gently for at least one hour, with regular stirring until thickened.

3. Just before serving the sauce, throw in the oregano and mix

CAUTION: the olives and salted capers season the sauce sufficiently so extra salt is not required.

METHOD (NAPOLI STYLE PIZZA)

1. In a frying pan, add olive oil to about ¼ inch depth and heat on medium to medium high. Roll out the pizza dough into circles about ¼ inch thick and 8 inch diameter.

2. Fry the pizzas for a few minutes each side until beginning to brown and puffed up.

3. Place the freshly fried pizza onto a plate, cover the pizza with the sauce and serve immediately.

Note: You may be wondering. What kind of a pizza is this? It looks nothing like any pizza I have seen before. So here's the reminder, this is Napoli style home cooking. Nonna used to cook this and call it pizza. Just try it and enjoy it for what it is!

MEAT TOMATO SAUCE

Approx total time: 2hr 15min

Our secret family sauce, no so secret any more! While it simmers, the ingredients get to know each other, and flavours come together and thicken up into a delicious sauce. This might be one of the most important recipes in this book since you can use this sauce to create for plenty of other dishes.

INGREDIENTS

- 500 Grams Good Quality Minced Beef
- 250 Grams Pork Rib On The Bone Cut Into Small Pieces
- 1 Can Peeled Plum Tomatoes
- 2 Tablespoons Tomato Puree
- Half Onion, Sliced
- 2 Cloves Garlic, Crushed
- 1 Tablespoon Freshly Chopped Parsley
- Extra Virgin Olive Oil
- 1 Bay Leaf
- 1 Cup Chicken Stock
- 2 Tablespoons Dried Oregano (Optional)
- 1 Cup Red Wine

METHOD

1. Fry the onion and garlic gently in olive oil in a sauce pan. Do not brown. When softened, add the meat and stir. Cook gently until the meat is browned.

2. Add the tomatoes, puree, red wine, stock, parsley, oregano (optional) and bay leaf. Mix thoroughly, crushing the plum tomatoes.

3. Cover the pan and simmer gently for 2 hours with regular stirring. The sauce will slowly thicken and take on a rich, dark red colour.

4. Can be served with cooked pasta. Add sufficient cooked pasta (300 gram pre-cooked weight) to the sauce in the pan, and stir in the sauce until all the pasta in covered. Serve.

    Can be also served with boiled rice or potato gnocchi. (See recipe for gnocchi on page 30)

POTATO PIE
Approx total time: 1hr 30min

This one usually gets devoured at the table since everyone loves it. But if you do have end up with leftovers it makes the best breakfast the morning after.

Not the best photo but this is a really delicious dish. This is best described as dense, crispy, creamy, savoury, cheesy and comforting. It's kind of like an alternative to lasagne. And it's easier to eat. The salami really packs a nice punch of flavour.

INGREDIENTS

- 4 Large Potatoes
- 2 Eggs, Beaten
- 1 Ball Mozzarella Cheese, Cut Into Small Pieces
- 100g Italian Salami, Preferably Napoli, Cut Into Small Pieces
- 2 Tablespoons Ground White Pepper
- Dried Breadcrumbs
- Salt To Season

METHOD

1. Clean the potatoes and boil in their skins. When soft, peel the potatoes and mash thoroughly. Add the cheese, beaten egg, salami salt and pepper to the mashed potato and mix.

2. Place the mixture into a round, deep oven dish, smooth out the top and sprinkle dried breadcrumbs of the top until well covered. Cover the dish and bake for at least 1 hour at 140C.

3. After this, remove the lid and return to the oven at 180°C (356°F / Gas Mark 4) for about 10 minutes to brown the breadcrumbs. Serve piping hot.

Goes well with pork chops and vegetables.

ROAST POTATOES IN GARLIC
Approx total time: 1hr 15min

Basically, it's a side dish of herb and garlic seasoned potatoes. What can I really say other than this is the perfect side dish to any main course which isn't high in carbohydrates. Don't serve it with pasta. Serve it with fish or roasted meats.

This one is cooked covered on low heat for a long time, this way they stay soft and retain moisture. They are then finished off uncovered so that they crisp up a little on the sides. It's potatoes. Just enjoy the ultimate comfort food they way humans have since the dawn of the potato.

INGREDIENTS

- 4 – 5 Medium Potatoes
- 1 Clove Garlic, Sliced
- 1/2 Onion, Well Chopped
- Teaspoon Thyme
- Teaspoon Rosemary
- Fresh, Chopped Parsley (Tablespoon)
- Extra Virgin Olive Oil (About 2 Tablespoons)
- Salt And Pepper To Taste

METHOD

1. Peel and slice the potatoes to about ¼ inch thickness. Place into an oven or casserole dish. Add the olive oil, onion, garlic and all other ingredients.

2. Thoroughly mix until all potatoes slices are covered in seasoning and oil. Cover, and cook for about 1 hour at 140°C (284°F / Gas Mark 1).

3. Remove the lid, turn up the heat to 180°C (356°F / Gas Mark 4) and cook until potatoes start to brown at the edges. Serve.

MINESTRONE

Approx total time: 1hr 20min

Minestrone is a vegetable soup / stew thing with some added beans. When visiting Nonna she would usually serve this as an appetiser or alongside a main course. We usually at this at family gatherings. A real comfort food this one. But also kinda fresh you can enjoy this one during winter or summer time.

The dish you see in the photo is the minestrone recipe as instructed in this book. However, I garnished mine with some additional chopped celery leaves. I usually garnish with uncooked leaves to add just a little additional freshness to the dish.

The secret of a good minestrone is to use well diced vegetables (about ¼ inch cubes) and a long cooking time on low heat.

INGREDIENTS

- 1 Courgette
- 1 Medium Potato, Peeled
- 1 Carrot, Peeled
- Spring Greens And / Or Spinach, Well Chopped
- Handful Of French Beans
- 3 – 4 Runner Beans
- 1 Medium Onion, Sliced
- 2 – 3 Cloves Garlic
- Fresh Parsley, Chopped (Two Tablespoons)
- 2 Tablespoons Tomato Puree
- 1.5 Litres Chicken Stock
- Extra Virgin Olive Oil

METHOD

1. Use a large saucepan. Crush the garlic and fry together with the onion in olive oil.

2. Dice all the vegetables to ¼ inch pieces and add to the pan.

3. Stir the vegetables into the fried onion / garlic.

4. Add the chicken stock and puree, stir and bring to the boil.

5. Simmer for 1 hour, adding more stock if necessary. Serve with boiled rice.

BRODO (VEGETABLE BROTH WITH SOUP PASTA)

Approx total time: 1hr

Look, another soup, and why not? Maybe I should create a book that focuses entirely on soups after this one. Hmmmm :D

Italian brodo is a tasty vegetable broth made by simmering fresh veggies like carrots, celery, onions, and tomatoes with aromatic herbs such as parsley and thyme. Slow-cooking brings out the natural flavours, creating a rich base. I took a bit of a shortcut when when cooking this one to take the photo. I simply used a stock cube, water and tomato puree. Hey, it looks the same. Sorry not sorry.

We would usually cook this one more often on special occasions such as Christmas and serve it as a starter dish before the main course.

INGREDIENTS

- 1 Whole Potato, Peeled
- 1 Whole Carrot, Peeled
- 1 Corn Cob
- Spring Greens And / Or Spinach Leaves
- 1 Stalk Celery, Whole With Leaves
- 1 Whole Onion, Peeled
- 2 – 3 Cloves Peeled Garlic
- 1 Can Peeled Plum Tomatoes
- 2 Tablespoons Tomato Puree
- 1.5 Litres Chicken Stock
- ¼ Cup Extra Virgin Olive Oil

METHOD

1. Bring the stock to the boil and add all the vegetables, whole, to the pan. Simmer for 40 minutes.
2. Just before the end of cooking, add the olive oil to the broth.
3. Strain the broth, to remove the vegetables.
4. Serve the hot broth with cooked soup pasta shells or small noodles.

SCHNITZEL (NEAPOLITAN MILANESE)
Approx total time: 30min

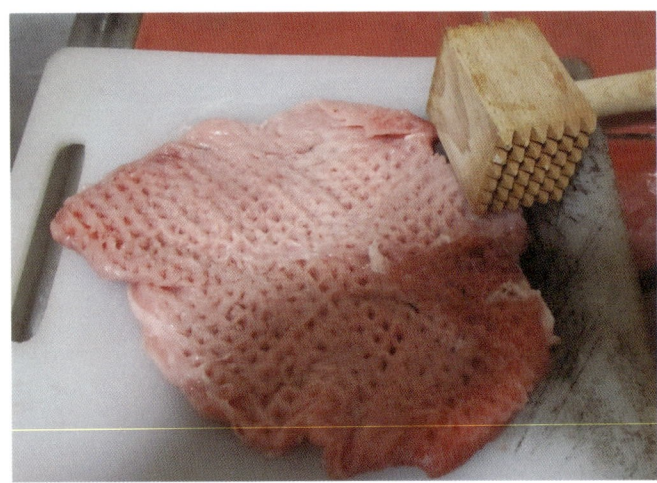

This one is really juicy and fresh. Don't skip on the pounding, it's essential. You may also want to squeeze some lemon juice on top once it's on the dinner table. Fry em up and make sure they are cooked well!

INGREDIENTS

- Boneless Pork Chops / Veal / Boneless Turkey Breast / Boneless Chicken Breast / Boneless Lamb Chops
- 2 Eggs, Beaten
- Flour
- Breadcrumbs
- Salt, Pepper
- Extra Virgin Olive Oil

METHOD

1. Tenderise the meat by banging with a meat tenderiser until the chop is thinned and flattened out to double size.

2. Coat each side of the tenderised chop with flour, place into beaten egg and then cover each side in a large saucepan with seasoned breadcrumbs.

3. Fry gently for a few minutes each side in olive oil until golden on both sides. Ensure that the meat is cooked thoroughly.

BEAN SOUP

Approx total time: 1hr 15min

The third soup in this book, and by they way there is no real order to these recipes. We use cannellini beans, it's not a mixed bean soup. It's kinda similar to minestrone, but some ingredients are different and the cooking method differs. This one is simmered for about 1 hour, slow cooked so that all those ingredients get to know each other.

Another comforting soup which can be severed as a starter or a main. There are no rules. Eat if for breakfast, at 3am or in a space ship.

INGREDIENTS

- 2 Cans Cannellini Beans Or 125g Dried Cannellini Beans Soaked Overnight In Warm Sodium Bicarbonate Solution
- Chicken Stock (1.5l)
- Chopped Onion
- Chopped Garlic
- Fresh Copped Parsley, 1 Tablespoon
- 2 Tablespoons Tomato Puree
- 1 Tin Peeled Plum Tomatoes
- 2 Stalks Celery, Chopped Including The Leaves
- Good Handful Of Oregano

METHOD

1. Fry the onion and garlic until softened. Do not brown.

2. If using pre-soaked dried beans, add all the ingredients, except the oregano, and simmer for about one hour or until the beans are tender.

3. If using canned beans, omit these until the last ten minutes of cooking.

4. Before serving, throw in the oregano. Serve.

FRIED GREEN LEAVES
Approx total time: 40min

Oh man, I really enjoyed this one. This one is pretty cheap to make, it's healthy and if you have a bad cold like I did at the time, the chilli peppers will clear your sinuses. Have plenty of tissues ready. If you can't find scarola leaves you can make this with pretty much any alternative leafy greens. Try it with kale, spinach, spring greens. They will all turn out pretty tasty.

The black olives and capers make this one quite interesting. Black olives are used more often in Napoli dishes. You may not need to add any additional salt since the olives and capers are already quite salty.

INGREDIENTS

- 500 Grams Scarola (Italian Endive) / Spinach / Spring Greens
- 200 Grams Black Olives, Pitted And Sliced
- Handful Of Salted Capers
- 1/2 Scotch Bonnet Chilli
- Two Cloves Garlic, Crushed
- 1/2 Onion, Sliced
- Extra Virgin Olive Oil

METHOD

1. Start by chopping the greens and add them to a large sauce pan of salted water. Cover the pan and set the stove to high heat. Bring the heat down to a gentle simmer before it reaches boiling point. Keep your eye on it.

2. While the greens are cooking finely dice the onion and chilli pepper and crush the garlic.

3. Add 2 to 3 tablespoons of olive oil to a frying pan and gently fry the onion, chilli pepper and garlic. Mix them together.

4. Add a 50ml of water to the frying pan and turn the heat to low. This helps prevent the garlic from burning.

5. Check on the greens, you want them to simmer for around 5 to 10 minutes.

6. Once the greens are soft drain the water and mix them with the oil in the frying pan.

7. Add the sliced olives and capers to the frying pan and mix them into the greens.

8. Allow to fry on medium to low heat for 20 minutes stirring occasionally. Add more olive oil if needed.

9. Enjoy.

RICE BALLS
Approx total time: 1hr 40min

Imagine cheesy meatballs but made with rice, salami and cheese coated in crispy breadcrumbs. That's basically what these are. They are one of my favourites, the salami and cheese taste great together. The best way I can describe this would be a pizza rice ball.

Tip for breadcrumbs: Breadcrumbs are quite expensive, so here's a life hack for you. Buy yourself a cheap brand of plain corn flakes. Pour them into a blender or crush them with in a mortar and pestle. One pack of cheap corn flakes is cheaper than breadcrumbs and makes a lot more.

INGREDIENTS

- 1 Cup Round Rice Or Other Sticky Rice
- 1 Ball Mozzarella, Chopped Into Small Pieces
- 2 Egg Yolks
- 2 Egg Whites
- 200g Chopped Italian Salami Such As Napoli
- Breadcrumbs
- Salt And Pepper To Taste
- Extra Virgin Olive Oil

METHOD

1. Cook the rice as per instructions and drain well. Allow to cool.

2. In a bowl, mix together the rice, egg yolks, cheese, salami, salt and pepper.

3. Form the mixture into golf ball sized balls. Dip each ball into the egg white and then cover with seasoned breadcrumbs.

4. Gently fry in olive oil until browned all over OR bake the balls in an oven for about 1 hour at 140°C (284°F / Gas Mark 1), followed by about 10 minutes at 180°C (356°F / Gas Mark 4) to brown the outsides. Serve.

These can be eaten as they are but the also go great when dipped into a spicy tomato sauce. See the next recipe.

SPICY TOMATO SAUCE

Approx total time: 1hr 30min

Not much I can say about this one. It's spicy tomato sauce. The secret to this one is the chicken stock, it mixes so well with the tomatoes. You can use chicken stock on any tomato sauce in place of salt and it will taste great. If you can't find Scotch Bonnet Chilli peppers you can always substitute them with a different chilli or chilli flakes.

INGREDIENTS

- 250ml Chicken Stock
- 1/2 Onion Chopped
- Two Cloves Garlic, Crushed
- Two Tablespoons Chopped Parsley
- 1 Can Peeled Plum Tomatoes
- Two Tablespoons Tomato Puree
- 1/2 Scotch Bonnet Chilli Pepper
- Handful Of Dried Oregano
- Extra Virgin Olive Oil

METHOD

1. Gently fry the onion, garlic and chilli pepper in olive oil in a saucepan.
2. Add the tomatoes and crush them with a fork.
3. Add the other ingredients except the oregano.
4. Gently simmer, with frequent stirring, for 1 hour until the sauce darkens and thickens.
5. Just before serving, throw in and mix the oregano.
6. Serve with spaghetti. Goes well with schnitzel (page 18)

MEAT BALLS
Approx total time: 1hr 30min

Delicious home-made meatballs: a perfect blend of beef, mozzarella, garlic, and Italian salami, ready to be fried or simmered in spicy tomato sauce. When you bite into these you might get a nice cheese pull.

INGREDIENTS

- 250 Grams Good Quality Minced Beef
- 1/2 Ball Mozzarella, Shredded
- 2 Cloves Garlic, Finely Chopped
- 2 Tablespoons Fresh Parsley, Chopped
- 100 Grams Italian Salami Cut Into Small Pieces
- 1 Beaten Egg
- Salt And Pepper
- Extra Virgin Olive Oil

METHOD

1. Mix all the ingredients thoroughly in a mixing bowl. Form into golf ball sized balls and either:

2. Fry gently in olive oil all sides until well browned all over; or:

3. Simmer for at least one hour in a spicy tomato sauce (see previous recipe)

GNOCCHI

Approx total time: 1hr (or overnight)

Gnocchi the way Nonna used to make it. I remember when I was a child she was teaching me how to pronounce it the Italian way ("gnyoh-kee" the G is almost silent but not quite)

You probably already know what Gnocchi is. But if not, here's the low-down. Gnocchi is a type of pasta. It's made from potatoes, flour, and eggs. The dough is then rolled into small dumplings.

It has a nice chewy texture and is quite delicious! Serve it with a tomato sauce of your choice and top it with cheese!

INGREDIENTS

- 4 – 5 Medium Sized Potatoes, Washed
- About 300 Grams Flour
- 2 Beaten Eggs
- Pinch Of Nutmeg
- Extra Virgin Olive Oil

METHOD

1. Boil the washed potatoes, in their skins, until soft. Drain and allow to cool for 30 minutes. Peel the potatoes and mash them well in a mixing bowl.

2. Add the beaten eggs and flour to the potatoes and mix until a dough is formed.

3. Add more flour if necessary until a firm but non-sticky dough is made. Knead well for 10 minutes on a lightly floured chopping board.

4. Cut of small balls on the dough and roll out into a long sausage shape, about 1/2 inch diameter.

5. Cut the strips into small pieces (about 1/2 inch) and lightly press each piece of gnocchi so that they are slightly thinner in the middle.

6. Spread out the gnocchi onto a large, lightly floured surface and sprinkle with flour.

7. Cover the gnocchi with tea towels and leave for at least one hour or preferable overnight to dry. Boil half a large pot full of salted water and add a half cup of olive oil.

8. When boiling, add the gnocchi all together into the pot and cook for a few minutes until they rise to the top of the pan.

9. Drain and serve well covered with a meat-tomato or spicy tomato sauce.

PEAS WITH ONION

Approx total time: 20min

This is a good way to add flavour to frozen peas. And yes I was quite reluctant to add this one because it's really overly simple. Nonna used to cook this as a side dish to serve along side other stuff. It's part of her recipes so we decided we should just add it for the sake of it.

Ingredients

- 250 Grams Frozen Peas
- 1 Small Onion, Chopped
- Extra Virgin Olive Oil
- Salt

Method

1. Gently fry the onion in the oil until softened.
2. Add the peas and stir well until the peas are covered in onion-oil.
3. Add water to just cover the peas. Add salt to taste.
4. Simmer in an open saucepan until the water has nearly all disappeared.
5. Serve.

ROAST FISH FILLETS
Approx total time: 45min

This one is covered in black olives and some capers. It may sound strange, but this is a lot more common in Napoli home cooking. We love our black olives. If you like black olives give this a try, you might be surprised how good it tastes. It's quite delicious!

Ingredients

- Three Boneless White Fish Fillets Such As Cod
- 50g Black Olives
- Handful Salted Capers
- Fresh Parsley
- Two Tablespoons Oregano
- Extra Virgin Olive Oil
- Pepper

Method

1. Sprinkle olive oil over the fish fillets in an oven dish.

2. Remove the stones from the olives, and slice.

3. Sprinkle the sliced olives, capers, oregano, chopped fresh parsley and pepper over the fillets.

4. Cover and allow to marinade for 1 hour in the refrigerator.

5. Cook in a heated oven at 190°C (375°F / Gas Mark 5) for about 30 – 40 minutes.

6. Drizzle with additional olive oil before serving.

    NOTE: the salted capers provide the salt seasoning. Do not add extra salt.

ROAST PORK CHOPS

Approx total time: 2hr 30min

Well this is a classic! Make sure you roast your pork chops covered in order to prevent them from turning dry. If cooked properly this are moist and juicy! If you don't have an oven dish with a lid you can wrap them in foil instead.

Another note, pork chops usually contain bone. If this annoys you as much as it annoys me you can always pork steaks instead.

INGREDIENTS

- 4 Pork Chops
- 2 Cloves Garlic, Sliced
- 1/2 Chopped Onion
- Few Sprigs Of Rosemary And Thyme
- Chopped Fresh Parsley
- Extra Virgin Olive Oil
- Salt And Pepper To Taste

METHOD

1. Cut grooves into the pork chops. Insert slices of garlic into the grooves.

2. Sprinkle the other ingredients onto the chops.

3. Sprinkle with olive oil, cover and let marinate in the fridge for 1 hour to overnight.

4. Gently roast the cops in a covered oven dish at 140°C (284°F / Gas Mark 1) for 1 hour, uncover, and cook for a further 10 minutes at 180C.

POTATOES IN TOMATO AND GARLIC

Approx total time: 1hr 30min

More potatoes, and comforting they are. Mouth watering and delicious, treat yourself and your loved ones to the flavours of roasted potatoes in tomatoes and garlic sauce, because every meal should be a moment of joy!

Here's a comfort food that is perfect for a cold winter night! I kinda regret putting this on a red plate, Would have looked way better on a white plate. The photography is a learning process, go easy on me.

INGREDIENTS

- 4 Medium Potatoes, Peeled
- 2 Cloves Crushed Garlic
- 1/2 Onion, Sliced
- 1 Can Peeled Plum Tomatoes
- 1 Cup Chicken Stock
- 2 Tables Spoons Fresh Parsley, Chopped
- Handful Of Oregano
- Salt & Pepper

METHOD

1. Slice the potatoes into ¼ inch thick slices and spread them evenly in an oven dish.

2. Add layers of onions, tomatoes, and parsley on top of the potatoes.

3. Mix crushed garlic with chicken stock, then pour it over the potatoes. Make sure the potatoes are covered by the liquid, but leave some parts of onion and tomato uncovered.

4. Oven cook uncovered at 180°C (356°F / Gas Mark 4) for about 90 minutes. Check and stir every 25 to 30 minutes. Your meal is ready when the sauce thickens, and the potatoes become soft.

5. Just before serving, toss in the oregano, mix, and season to taste with salt and pepper.
Enjoy your delicious dish!

COURGETTE / AUBERGINE (EGGPLANT) IN EGG BATTER

Approx total time: 30min

These crispy slices are perfect as a side dish or a quick snack. They're made by frying thin slices of courgette and eggplant until they're golden and delicious.

The olive oil adds a fruity flavour that makes them even tastier. It's an easy recipe that's really satisfying to eat.

INGREDIENTS

- 1 Courgette
- 1 Large Egg Plant Or (Preferable) 3 – Chinese / Japanese Eggplants
- 1 To 2 Beaten Eggs
- Flour
- Salt And Pepper
- Extra Virgin Olive Oil

METHOD

1. Wash the courgettes and eggplants, cut in half and slice length-ways into slices about 1/8th inch thick.

2. Cover both sides of each slice with seasoned flour and then dip into the beaten egg.

3. Leave in the egg for about 1 minute.

4. Gently fry the batter-covered slices in olive oil a few minutes each side until golden brown and soft.

PORK ONION PEPPER SAUCE FOR PASTA

Approx total time: 1hr

This sauce is packed with flavour! It's made by cooking juicy pork with lots of onions until everything is super tender. Then, we add chicken stock and pepper and let it simmer until it becomes rich and tasty.

Pour it over pasta, like penne or shells, and you've got a meal that's savoury, comforting, and absolutely delicious! Pretty tasty!

INGREDIENTS

- 300 Grams Cubed Pork
- 6 Medium Onions
- 1 Cup Chicken Stock
- 20 Grams White Pepper Powder
- 2 – 3 Tablespoons Extra Virgin Olive Oil

METHOD

1. Finely chop the onion and add all to a saucepan containing heated olive oil.

2. Gently cook for about 30 – 40 minutes until the onion is well softened but not browned.

3. Add the pork and stir. Add the stock and pepper and simmer gently for at least one hour until the sauce reduces.

4. Add the sauce to cooked 500 grams pasta such a penne, rigatoni or large shells.

5. Mix well to cover the pasta with the sauce.

TENDER FRIED PEPPERS

Approx total time: 1hr 30min

This dish is all about tender peppers fried up to perfection! We slice up yellow, red, and green peppers, then toss them in a pan with olives, capers, parsley, and a little kick from a Scotch bonnet pepper.

Cook it all together slowly until the peppers are super soft and bursting with flavour. Serve it with some crusty white bread for a tasty and healthful meal!

INGREDIENTS

- 1 Each Of Yellow, Red And Green Pepper
- 100 Grams Black Olives, De-Stoned
- Handful Salted Capers
- Two Tables Spoons Fresh Parsley, Chopped
- Half Scotch Pepper
- Salt And Pepper To Taste
- Extra Virgin Olive Oil

METHOD

1. Gently heat ¼ inch olive oil in a frying pan.

2. Cut the peppers into 4 pieces each and de-seed. Add to the frying pan and stir to coat the peppers in olive oil. Gently fry with regular stirring.

3. Slice the olives and scotch pepper. Add all the remaining ingredients to the pan (capers, olives, scotch bonnet pepper, parsley) and stir in.

4. Add salt (sparingly because the salted capers add salt) and ground pepper to taste.

5. Cook gently, with regular stirring, for about 1 hour until the peppers are very soft.

6. Serve with crusty white bread.

This is like a viral life hack video. So if you're like me and many other people, you always make a massive porting of spaghetti bolognese. So you have leftovers the next day and you can transform it into a new crispy dish using some eggs and olive oil. Pretty straight forward and it tastes really good.

This is the real life cheat code in action. Your guests will think you're a nut case and they will love you for it. Never say never, be experimental and enjoy yourself.

FRIED LEFT OVER SPAGHETTI BOLOGNESE

Approx total time: 30min

If you have left over spaghetti bolognese, this is a good method for making a quick tasty alternative.

METHOD

1. Beat two eggs and stir into the spaghetti.

2. Moderately heat olive oil in a frying pan.

3. Add the spaghetti-egg mixture and fry over moderate heat for about 15 minutes until the bottom becomes brown to near black.

4. Put a large plate over the frying pan and flip the spaghetti onto the plate.

5. Then slide the spaghetti back into the frying pan and cook the other side until very well browned.

6. Serve.

GARLIC TOAST

Approx total time: 15min

I was sceptical about this one but after making it I was surprised to find that this works very well. Too well in fact. This is better than garlic bread. The method is stupidly simple but the toast really does absorb a strong garlic flavour.

You can just have this as a quick snack, but if you want to be a bit more classy use an expensive sourdough bread and serve it along side a soup for dipping.

You see those two cuts of raw garlics on the plate? I totally ate them raw after taking the photo. It's good for you.

INGREDIENTS

- 2 Slices Toasted Bread
- 1 Clove Garlic Cut Into Two
- Salt
- Pepper
- Oregano
- Extra Virgin Olive Oil

METHOD

1. Get your self some nice bread and toast it. (I usually go for sourdough)

2. Sprinkle or brush olive oil onto the toast. Cover the whole surface.

3. Rub each piece of toast with garlic, all over.

4. Sprinkle with oregano, salt and pepper.

5. Eat!

    Eat it n it's own or serve it with soup. It may be simple but It tastes a lot better than you may think. Just try it!

NAPOLI STYLE LASAGNE

Approx total time: 3hr

For this one you will want to make the sauce first and heave it ready. See page 8 for Nonna's style meat tomato sauce or page 56 for a traditional ragù.

INGREDIENTS

- 1 Large Pot Of Meat-Tomato Sauce (See Previous Recipe)
- 6 – 8 Sheets Fresh Lasagne Pasta, Cooked And Cooled (See Below)
- 2 Hard Boiled Eggs, Sliced
- 100g Sliced Napoli Salami, Each Piece Cut Into Quarters
- 4 Slices Cooked Ham
- 2 Balls Mozzarella, Sliced

INGREDIENTS (FRESH LASAGNE PASTA SHEETS)

- About 500g Flour
- Teaspoon Salt
- 4 To 6 Eggs
- Extra Virgin Olive Oil

METHOD (PASTA SHEETS)

1. Mix all ingredients together to make a dough. Add more flour / eggs as necessary to obtain an elastic, but not sticky, dough. Knead on a floured surface for at least 10 minutes. Cover with a tea towel and leave for about 30 minutes.

2. Removes small balls of dough and roll out on a floured surface into oval shaped sheets, about 1/8th inch thick and large enough to fit snugly into an over dish (e.g. about 10 inches length, 6 inches wide). The exact shape does not matter since the pasta sheets will take on the shape of the oven dish during cooking in the oven.

3. Bring a large pot of salted water to the boil and add a tablespoon of olive oil to prevent the pasta sticking together. Add each sheet to the boiling water 2 – 3 at a time and cook for about 1 minute until the sheets rise to the top. Remove the cooked pasta and place into a bowl of cold water.

METHOD (LAYERING THE LASAGNE)

1. Spread a layer of meat-tomato sauce over the bottom of a medium sized oven dish. Take a sheet of cooked pasta and place over the sauce, pressing down gently.

2. Spread some more sauce over the sheet of pasta. Add sliced mozzarella to cover the sheet. Then layer sliced boiled egg over the cheese. Add another layer of sauces to cover the egg and cheese.

3. Add a second sheet of cooked pasta and gently press down. Repeat as for the first layer except add salamis pieces instead of sliced egg over the cheese. Add the third sheet and repeat but this time with sliced ham over the cheese.

4. Repeat this process using all the sheets of pasta and adding layers on sliced boiled egg, salami and ham over the mozzarella for each layer.

5. Cover the dish loosely with kitchen foil. Bake in the oven at 160°C (320°F / Gas Mark 3) for 1 – 1.5 hours until well cooked throughout. Remove the kitchen foil, raise the temperature to 180°C (356°F / Gas Mark 4) and cook for a further 10 – 15 minutes. Take out of the oven and allow to rest for 10 minutes. Serve!

CHICKEN DIAVOLO

Approx total time: 1hr

Hmmmm, delicious… this is a garlic and pepper roasted chicken dish, it's succulent, juicy and tender. Guaranteed to restore your HP (fans of rpgs will understand)

The secret? Slow-roasting at a low temperature ensures that every inch of the chicken cooks evenly, while also crisping up that irresistible skin. Please make sure the meat is cooker before serving!

INGREDIENTS

- 2 Chicken Quarters
- 4 Cloves Garlic, Sliced
- Juice Of One Lemon
- Salt
- Plenty Of Ground Black Pepper
- Extra Virgin Olive Oil

METHOD

1. Make small cuts all over the chicken pieces.

2. Insert sliced garlic into the cuts.

3. Drizzle with olive oil.

4. Pour the lemon juice over the chicken.

5. Sprinkle salt and then add plenty of ground black pepper until the chicken is generously covered.

6. Roast in a low oven 150°C (302°F / Gas Mark 2) until thoroughly cooked and the skin has become crispy.

That's it for Nonna's recipes. The next lot of recipes are popular with her grandson. Starting with the classic tomato sauce!

CLASSIC TOMATO SAUCE
Approx total time: 2hr 30min

What can I say about this? This is lain and simple tomato sauce. Sometimes it is the simple recipes that are the best, things don't need to be overly complicated.

You could argue that this isn't "pure tomato sauce" since it contains other ingredients too. This recipe is however very flavourful and authentic Italian.

There are no concrete rules, the cooking methods may differ from home to home. If you want pure tomato sauce you can create just that! Simply chop up a load of fresh tomatoes and cook them covered on low heat for a few hours until the sauce thickens. Keep checking back to stir and crush them and make sure nothing burns at the bottom. This will give you tomato sauce in its purest form.

Ingredients

- 5kg Of Peeled Plum Tomatoes. Or Feel Free To Experiment With Different Tomato Varieties
- 1 Red, Green Or Yellow Bell Pepper
- 2 Tablespoons Of Rock Salt
- 2 Cloves Of Garlic, Crushed
- A Handful Of Fresh Basil Leaves
- Extra Virgin Olive Oil
- Jars To Store The Sauce In

Method

1. Chop up the bell pepper and remove the seeds and stem.

2. Put the bell pepper into a blender and add your tomatoes (as many as you can fit in). Make sure you blend all of your tomatoes, do it in batches if need be.

3. Blend everything together until smooth.

4. Add 4 to 5 tablespoons of extra virgin olive oil into a large saucepan along with your crushed garlic heat gently and stir.

5. After about 1 or 2 minutes pour about 100ml of water into the saucepan.

6. Next add in your blended tomatoes mix into the saucepan.

7. Now allow the tomatoes to cook on low to medium heat for 2 hours or until it starts to thicken up. Keep checking back to stir it every 15 minutes.

8. The longer you cook the sauce the more flavour it will have. Once you are happy with the thickness of your sauce turn the heat off and allow it to cool down.

9. Taste test your sauce for salt and adjust to your liking.

10. Next chop up your fresh basil leaves and mix them into your sauce along.

11. Add a bit more extra virgin olive oil and mix it in. About 2 to 3 tablespoons.

12. Store your sauce in the fridge in jars or tubs. Consume within 2 days.

AUTHENTIC RAGÙ / BOLOGNESE SAUCE WITH PASTA

Approx total time: 2hr to 5hr (the longer you cook the better)

Authentic ragù or Bolognese sauce demands patience to achieve desired flavours and thickness.

INGREDIENTS

- 1 Diced Onion (Red Or Brown)
- 3 Fine Diced Celery Sticks
- 2 Grated Carrots
- Salt And Pepper
- Tomato Paste 150g
- 400g Of Peeled Plum Tomatoes
- 1 Litre Of Passata
- Extra Virgin Olive Oil
- Minced Meat, 400g Beef Mince, 400g Pork Mince And 200g Veal Mice
- Red Wine
- Pasta (I Used Spaghetti But Pappardelle Is Best!)
- An Italian Grated Hard Cheese Of Choice
- Extra Virgin Olive Oil

METHOD

1. Add extra virgin olive oil to a large pot and allow to heat on medium low for a minute, then add the onions and allow them to cook for a couple of minutes.

2. Add the diced celery and grated carrot, mix together with the onions. After a few minutes add half a cup of red wine and allow it to cook until the liquid has almost fully evaporated

3. Now add the all of your minced meat, beef, pork and veal. Mix and stir and allow it to cook until it turns grey. Season with salt and pepper while cooking.

4. Keep cooking the meat until any liquids at the bottom are evaporated. Then add another half cup or red wine. As before, all this too cook until the red wine has evaporated.

5. Add the tomato passata, peeled plum tomatoes and tomato paste, mix everything together. Then add half a cup of water and mix again. At this point you you need to play the waiting game.

6. Do not cover, and leave to simmer on low heat for 2 to 5 hours. Come back to stir and mix every 20 to 30 minutes. The longer you cook the better it will taste. Top up with water as necessary.

7. Keep cooking and once you are happy your sauce is almost ready. You want the sauce to be thick and not watery or runny. Taste it for seasoning and add salt and pepper to taste.

8. Next you want to cook your pasta. Bring a saucepan if salted water to the boil and cook your spaghetti for 9 to 10 minutes. Or follow the instructions on the packet but subtract one minute from the cooking time.

9. Use a cup to scoop a cup of pasta water, you will need this to help combine the sauce with the pasta. Drain the rest of the water.

10. Now you want to add the pasta to the bolognese sauce and mix everything together. Add about half a cup of the pasta water and keep mixing on a low heat. At this point you need to use your own judgment as to if you want to add more pasta water or not. You want your sauce to be thick and creamy. If you add too much pasta water keep it cooking while mixing on low heat until the consistency is to your liking.

11. Your authentic ragù pasta dish is ready to serve. Optionally top with an Italian grated hard cheese and some fresh basil leaves.
    ENJOY!

BASIL PESTO
Approx total time: 20min

I love making home made pesto. And I have a confession to make about this photo. The recipe to the right is the correct recipe, however, I didn't have pine nuts, and since pine nuts are kinda expensive and I have rent to pay, I used peanuts instead. And I used a cheaper Italian grated cheese in place of the parmesan.

It matters not, still looks the same and what can I say, it's ok to substitute ingredients. You can make delicious pesto using pistachio nuts to. So don't be afraid to experiment once you have the techniques down.

INGREDIENTS

- 1 Cup Of Fresh Basil Leaves
- 3 Tablespoons Of Grated Parmesan
- 1 Clove Of Garlic
- 10g Of Pine Nuts
- Extra Virgin Olive Oil
- Rock Salt
- Mortar And Pestle

METHOD

1. Pour 3 to 4 tablespoons of olive oil into the mortar along with your basil leaves.

2. Use the pestle to crush and mix the leaves and oil together into a paste.

3. Now add the garlic and do the same, crush it into a paste and mix it in.

4. Next your add your pine nuts and once again crush and mix them into the paste.

5. At this point if the paste is looking too thick add a couple more tablespoons of olive oil. You may prefer your pesto to be thicker or runnier. It's your choice.

6. Now add the grated parmesan cheese into the paste and mix it together.

7. Finally, taste test and add salt or more parmesan to taste.

8. Your pest is ready! I recommend you consume it immediately. Or if you can store it In a sealed glass jar in the refrigerator and consume within 2 days.

Pesto can be turned into a delicious pasta dish. See the next recipe for details.

PESTO PASTA (GEMELLI AL PESTO)
Approx total time: 20min

I love this one for its simplicity and it sticks together nice and firm. It's quite a small dish so I recommend you serve this as an appetiser.

And here's a pro tip: to give your dish that picture-perfect dome shape, simply press it into a small bowl, place a plate on top, and flip – just like making a sand castle! So go ahead, whip up this crowd-pleaser and prepare to wow your guests with your culinary skills!

INGREDIENTS

- 1 Cup Of Freshly Made Pesto
- 200g Gemelli Pasta
- Grated Parmesan Cheese
- A Couple Of Basil Leaves
- Rock Salt
- Pepper

METHOD

1. Start by boiling water in a medium sized saucepan. Add about 2 tablespoons of salt.

2. Add your gemelli pasta to the boiling water and set your timer for 9 minutes Stir occasionally.

3. Once the timer is up taste test your pasta ti make sure it's at the constancy that you like.

4. Drain the water but keep half a cup of the pasta water.

5. Now return the pan to low heat and mix in your pesto with the pasta. Add a few drops of pasta water. Mix and stir it together. (Optional: Add some cracked black pepper to taste.)

6. Your Gemelli Al Pesto is ready to serve. To get that dome like shape that you see in the picture see the caption under the picture.

7. Optionally top your pasta with grated parmesan cheese and garnish with a couple of basil leaves.

8. Enjoy.

CAPRESE SALAD

Approx total time: 15min

The vibrant hues mirroring the Italian flag are eloquently captured in the classic Caprese Salad, making it an ideal choice as either an attractive looking side salad or a tasteful appetizer preceding the main course.

INGREDIENTS

- 1 Or 2 Balls Of Buffalo Mozzarella
- 1 Or 2 Large Fresh Beef Tomatoes
- A Handful Of Large Fresh Basil Leaves
- Dried Oregano
- Extra Virgin Olive Oil
- Salt And Pepper
- Round Plate Or Platter

METHOD

1. Slice the Tomato and Mozzarella into 1 to 2 cm thick slices. You want the Tomato and Mozzarella to be roughly the same thickness

2. First place down a slice of tomato on the edge of the plate, season it with salt, pepper and oregano.

3. Next place a basil leaf on top of the tomato slice.

4. Now on top of the basil leaf and covering 50% of the tomato place a slice of mozzarella.

5. Next you place another slice of tomato on top of the mozzarella covering 50% followed by a basil leaf and another slice of seasoned tomato.

6. Repeat this process around the plate, once you have complete a full circle do the same in the middle so that it spirals inward.

7. Once the plate is covered lightly drizzle olive oil over your salad.

8. Your perfect starter dish is ready to serve!

AUTHENTIC CARBONARA

Approx total time: 30min

The Classic! Carbonara, is a dish that is loved in Rome, it features spaghetti and is accompanied with a cheesy egg sauce. The result is rich and creamy. Season it with a lot of pepper. If you think you've added a lot of pepper, keep on grinding for another 20 times, you want it to look like it's at least 50% covered in pepper. It's really filling, don't eat it every day. Eat it in moderation for the sake of your heart.

INGREDIENTS

- 300g Spaghetti
- 150g Guanciale (Or Pancetta)
- 4 Eggs (Or 6 Egg Yolks)
- 200g Grated Pecorino Cheese
- Pepper

METHOD

1. Start by cutting the Guanciale (or Pancetta) into small long strips. About a quarter length of our finger. Like in the photo to the left.

2. Add the Guanciale to a frying pan and cook on medium to low heat until it starts to bring and turn crispy. Note, you won't need to add oil, the fat from the meat will be sufficient. Once it starts to brown you can turn the heat down to the lowest setting on the smallest ring and move on to the next step.

3. Add your spaghetti into boiling water and set your timer for 9 minutes (or one minute less than the instructions on the packet)

4. While the spaghetti is cooking add all of your eggs into a mixing bowl and beat them until smooth and thoroughly mixed.

5. Now add all 200g of the pecorino cheese into the eggs and mix it together to form a creamy paste. Then season with a lot of black pepper and mix in one more time.

6. Use a cup to scoop out a full cup of pasta water from the cooking spaghetti and add about ¼ of a cup of the pasta water to your egg and cheese mix. Mix it together.

7. Once the spaghetti is done drain the water and mix it together with the Guanciale and pour your creamy egg and cheese mix into it. Make sure you keep mixing it together on low heat.

8. For the last step, add another half cup of pasta water and mix everything together on the lowest possible heat setting. Keep stirring, you don't want the egg to turn into scrambled egg, but rather you want the pasta water, cheese and eggs to mix together into a tick and creamy sauce. If you're feeling confident give it a toss!

9. Once you are happy with the consistency of the sauce your Carbonara is ready to serve. Top with pepper and additional hard cheese to taste.

10. Enjoy!

LENTILS PASTA

Approx total time: 45min

INGREDIENTS

- 1 Cup Of Conchiglie Pasta (I Mixed Mine With Fusilli In The Photo)
- 1 Or 2 Cans Of Cooked Lentils (Any Type)
- 1 Diced Carrot, 1 Chopped Stick Of Celery, Half A Diced Onion
- 2 Cloves Of Crushed Garlic
- 2 – 3 Sticks Of Fresh Rosemary
- 1 Litre Vegetable Stock
- Classic Tomato Sauce (See Page 54)
- Extra Virgin Olive Oil
- Salt And Pepper
- Salami Cut Into Cubes (Or Guanciale / Pancetta)

METHOD

1. Add 5 tablespoons to a large cooking pot and heat on medium heat. Add the diced onion, carrots and celery.

2. Stir and cook. After 3 minutes add a few drops of vegetable stock to help prevent burning the ingredients.

3. Add now add the 2 cloves of crushed garlic and your sticks of rosemary. Add another 50ml to 100ml of stock, stir and cook for a further 4 minutes.

4. Now add the Salami and cook for a further 3 to 4 minutes. Keep stirring and mixing!

5. Now it's time to add your lentils and mix everything together for a minute. Add the rest of your vegetable stock and bring to a simmer.

6. Add 5 – 10 tablespoons of tomato sauce depending on how much tomato flavour you want to add. Stir it in. Put the lid on the pot and allow it to cook on medium to low heat for 5 to 10 minutes.

7. Keep an eye on the lentils, if liquid levels are getting low top it up with some water.

8. Fish out the rosemary sticks, add your soup pasta and stir it in. It will absorb the stock quickly, if it's looking quite dry top it up with some water until all the pasta is just about submerged in liquid. Put the lid back on and allow to simmer for 5 minutes.

9. Now remove the lid and stir everything again . Make sure nothing is stuck at the bottom.

10. Taste test the pasta to make sure it is cooked to your liking. You'll need to use your judgment at this point if you need to add more water. The aim is to allow the pasta to absorb all the liquid so that you are left with a thick lentil sauce. Keep stirring.

11. Season with salt and pepper to taste. Make sure you taste test first!

12. Taste test again, once you are happy take it off the heat. Stir everything together and allow it to rest for 2 minutes.

13. Your Lentil pasta is ready to serve. Optionally you can top with an Italian hard cheese. Eat while it's still hot!

KALE & OLIVES PASTA

Approx total time: 30min

Here's something a bit more healthful. If you're like me then you love your green leaves. Ideally use kale but you can experiment and use cabbage, spring greens or any other green leaves of your choice. The black olives are back with this one, they just work so well in Napoli style cooking. It goes without saying, if you don't like it spicy just leave out the chillies.

Eat plenty of green leaves, it's good for you! And don't skimp on the pepper!

INGREDIENTS

- 2 Or 3 Cups Of Chopped Kale
- 300 Grams Of Fusilli Pasta
- 30 Pitted And Chopped Black Olives
- 2 To 3 Fine Chopped Garlic Cloves
- Chilli Flakes
- Rock Salt
- Pepper
- Extra Virgin Olive Oil

METHOD

1. Bring a saucepan of generously salted water to the boil and add the chopped kale and pasta. They cook together. Set your timer for 10 minutes.

2. Add four tablespoons of olive oil to a deep frying pan. Heat on low and add the chopped garlic and olives.

3. Take a tablespoon of the pasta water and add it to the garlic in the frying pan to prevent it from burning.

4. Add a the chilli flakes to the frying pan and stir everything together. Leave it on low heat.

5. Once the timer is up take a cup and scoop out some pasta water from the saucepan and drain the rest.

6. Add the pasta and kale to the frying pan and mix in with the garlic and olive base. Top with pepper.

7. Now for the final step add half a cup of your pasta water into the frying pan and mix. Keep the heat on low and stir allowing the pasta water to evaporate slowly turn into a light sauce. If confident give it a toss so that everything mixes together nicely. If your frying pan has a lid use it while tossing to prevent spillage.

8. Your dish is ready to serve. Top with more pepper and chilli flakes to taste.

9. Enjoy!

CREAMY MUSHROOM AND CASHEW PASTA

Approx total time: 30min

This is one of my earliest recipes. I took that photo back in 2016, I didn't really know what I was doing back then but the photo turned out really well. I've finally used it for something. The dish is really tasty too.

INGREDIENTS

- Extra Virgin Olive Oil
- 2 Cloves Of Crushed Garlic
- 1 Cup Of Cashew Nuts (Salted Or Unsalted)
- 2 Cups Of Sliced Mushrooms (Whatever Mushrooms You Like)
- Spaghetti (Or A Pasta Of Your Choice)
- Dried Mixed Herbs
- Whiskey (Optional)
- Fresh Watercress
- 1/2 Cup Single Cream
- Parmesan Cheese (Grated)
- Salt & Pepper

METHOD

1. Start by filling a saucepan with water and add 1 tablespoon of sea salt. Put it on the hob on medium to high heat.

2. While the water is heating add 1 tablespoons of olive oil to a frying pan and add your crushed garlic. Cook for 1 minute on medium low heat.

3. Add the mushrooms and cashews to the frying pan. Stir frequently and allow them to fry until the mushrooms start to brown.

4. By this point the water should be boiling, add your pasta to the water and set your timer for 10 minutes or follow the instructions on the packet.

5. Pour 1 small shot glass (about 25ml) of whiskey into your mushrooms and mix in. Allow the liquid and alcohol to boil off.

6. Next pour your cream into the mushrooms and cashews and mix.

7. Next add your grated parmesan cheers into the creamy mushrooms. How much cheese you use is up to you.

8. Mix and stir until you have a nice thick and creamy mushroom and cashew sauce.

9. Taste test, and add salt and pepper to taste. You should also add your mixed herbs now.

10. Your pasta should be cooked by this point. Scoop out some pasta water in a mug and set it aside. Drain the rest of the water and add the pasta to the creamy mushroom sauce.

11. Mix the pasta into the sauce, if it's starting to look dry or not mixing very well add a bit of pasta water and mix together.

12. Your dish is ready to serve. Top it with more parmesan and pepper and garnish with watercress.

13. Serve immediately.

CREAMY BROCCOLI PASTA
Approx total time: 25min

Another healthy one, if you love broccoli and cheese then you'll love this! It's nice and creamy thanks to the use of pasta water. Remember, pasta water is your friend. Always save a cup for the final mixing!

INGREDIENTS

- 300g To 400g Broccoli
- 300g Farfalle Pasta
- 2 Cloves Of Crushed Garlic
- Extra Virgin Olive Oil
- Grated Pecorino Cheese (To Taste)
- Rock Salt And Pepper

METHOD

1. Cut up the broccoli into bite sized pieces. If eating the stem cut it into small pieces so it cooks well.

2. Add the broccoli to salted boiling water and allow it to cook for approx 6 minutes.

3. Add 4 to 5 tablespoons of olive oil to a frying pan and also add your 2 cloves of crushed garlic and gently cook the garlic on low heat. Add an additional tablespoon of water to help prevent the garlic from burning.

4. After the broccoli has been cooking for 6 minutes turn the heat to low and scoop it out of the pan and into the frying pan using a sieve. Keep the water!

5. Now add your pasta to the saucepan into the water used to cook the broccoli. Turn the heat back up and set your timer for 10 minutes or follow the instructions on the packet.

6. While the pasta is cooking stir the broccoli so that it mixes with the olive oil and garlic. Season the broccoli with salt and pepper to taste.

7. When the pasta has cooked use a mug to scoop out half a cup of pasta water. You will need it!

8. Now strain the pasta and transfer the spaghetti to your frying pan. Mix it together with the broccoli and oil. While mixing on low medium add about ¼ of a cup of your pasta water and keep stirring until the sauce thickens up to desired thickness.

9. Finally add your grated pecorino cheese into the mix, however much you like but be careful, it is quite a salty cheese!

10. While in the bowl drizzle with olive oil and top with some more pecorino. Serve and eat!

ITALIAN STYLE PICKLED EGGS

Approx total time: 30min + 4 to 6 days to pickle

I feel like I'm scraping the barrel with this one, but they taste good and it's fun to pickle your own eggs.

Balsamic vinegar-pickled eggs not only look cool and offer a tangy taste, but they also boast a dark and fancy appearance that adds a touch of class. I mean look at them. They look like some kind of precious stone. Until you slice them in half, in which case they just look like a boiled egg.

These are quite useful. I picked about 15 eggs at one in my pickle jar. They lasted around 10 days and I was sick of eating picked eggs by the end of it. But you may love picked eggs or have guests over, in which case they will go pretty quickly.

INGREDIENTS

- A Glass Jar With Lid, Big Enough To Hold 6 Hard Boiled Eggs.
- 6 Hard Boiled Eggs
- 1 Diced Onion
- 5 Cloves Of Crushed Garlic
- 1 Cup Of Italian Balsamic Vinegar
- 1 Cup Of Water
- Peppercorns
- Rock Salt
- Mixed Dried Herbs (Basil, Oregano, Thyme, Rosemary)

METHOD

1. Bring a pan of water to the boil and slowly lower your eggs into the boiling water using a ladle.

2. Next we need to prepare the pickle juice. Get yourself a pan. A milk pan would be ideal for easy pouring.

3. While the eggs are cooking dice an onion and crush 5 cloves of garlic.

4. Measure out 1 cup of balsamic vinegar and 1 cup of water.

5. Add your ingredients into the milk pan pan and set the heat to medium.

6. While the vinegar is heating add 1 tablespoon of peppercorns, 1 tablespoon of your mixed dried herbs and 1 tablespoon of rock salt. Leave it on low heat to simmer.

7. By this point your eggs should be hard boiled (approx 12 – 15 minutes of boiling)

8. Remove the eggs pan from the heat and now add cold water from the tap. Drain and top up fully with cold water again. Repeat until the water no longer heats up so that are submerged in cold water. Leave the eggs to stand in cold water for 10 minutes.

9. Now peel your eggs and put them into your pickle jar. The eggs should peel much easier when cold. You can peel them while under water to make it even easier.

10. Take your balsamic vinegar off the heat and allow it to cool down. Once it has cooled down pour it over your hard boiled eggs into the pickle jar.

11. Put the jar into the refrigerator and allow the eggs to pickle for 4 to 6 days.

Kale and Salami Omelette

Approx total time: 20min

This is a bit like a pizza omelette. Treat it as if you're cooking a pizza. You may want to add some chopped black olives too. Serve it alongside marinated olives (next recipe) and you've got yourself a quick and tasty lunch!

INGREDIENTS

- 3 – 4 Eggs
- 30g To 50g Italian Salami
- 1 Crushed Clove Of Garlic
- 1 Cup Of Chopped Kale
- 2 Tablespoons Butter
- 1 Ball Of Fresh Mozzarella (Sliced)
- Fine Chopped Fresh Parsley
- Salt And Pepper To Taste

METHOD

1. Finely slice the kale, ensuring it is not too small.

2. In a frying pan, evenly distribute butter and add the chopped kale. Fry on medium-low heat.

3. While the kale cooks, thinly slice the salami and add it to the pan. Allow additional fat to render from the salami.

4. Crush garlic and stir it into the pan. Reduce heat to low.

5. Crack and whisk the eggs in a bowl or measuring jug. Add finely chopped parsley, and season with salt and pepper to taste. Stir well, considering the existing salt content from the salami and butter.

6. Pour the egg mixture into the pan and allow it to cook gently.

7. While the omelette is cooking, thinly slice the ball of mozzarella and layer it over the top.

8. Once the omelette is mostly cooked, remove the pan from heat and place it under the grill to cook the top. The omelette is ready when the surface egg has cooked, and the mozzarella has browned slightly.

9. Enjoy your delicious omelette!

Marinated Olives

Approx total time: 10min

I've left olives to last, I'm really happy with the way the photo turned out. Creating this book has been a learning process in food photography as well as, err, creating a book for the first time... Anyway, look how colourful they are!

It's no secret that Italians tend to love olives. They are great they way they are, but you can take it to the next level by seasoning them with with olive oil, herbs, lemon and garlic. These are better than what you may be served in a restaurant, seriously, try this along side your main course. A luxury, this is gourmet stuff.

INGREDIENTS

- 2 Cups Mixed Olives (Such As Kalamata, Green, And Black)
- 2 Cloves Garlic, Thinly Sliced
- 1 Tablespoon Fresh Rosemary, Chopped
- 1 Tablespoon Fresh Thyme Leaves
- 1 Teaspoon Dried Oregano
- 1 Teaspoon Dried Basil
- 1/4 Teaspoon Red Pepper Flakes (Optional)
- Zest Of 1 Lemon
- Zest Of 1 Orange
- 1/4 Cup Extra Virgin Olive Oil
- Salt And Pepper To Taste

METHOD

1. Rinse the olives under cold water and drain well. Place them in a mixing bowl.

2. Add the sliced garlic, chopped rosemary, thyme leaves, dried oregano, dried basil, red pepper flakes (if using), lemon zest, and orange zest to the olives.

3. Drizzle the extra virgin olive oil over the olive mixture.

4. Season with salt and pepper to taste.

5. Toss everything together until the olives are well coated with the herbs, spices, and olive oil.

6. Cover the bowl and refrigerate the olives for at least 2 hours to allow the flavours to meld together.

7. Before serving, let the olives come to room temperature. Adjust seasoning if necessary.

8. Serve the Italian marinated mixed olives as an appetizer or as part of a charcuterie board. Enjoy!

USEFUL TIPS

Pasta Quality:
You can cook a delicious meal with any pasta. However, if you want to go that extra mile make sure you choose a good quality pasta. Good quality pasta is usually lighter in colour and has a grainy texture. The lesser quality pastas have a dark yellow colour with a smoother surface. Not only does the Good quality pasta taste better, thanks to it's grainy texture sauces stick to it better and it absorbs more flavours.

Additionally lighter, grainy pasta often indicates a higher quality of durum wheat, which tends to retain more nutrients during the milling process. As a result, it can offer superior nutritional benefits compared to its darker counterpart, providing essential vitamins, minerals, and dietary fibre that contribute to a balanced diet. See the photos below to see the difference between good quality and poor quality.

Cheapo pasta

(I buy this one more often because money)

Quality pasta

(I buy this one when I can afford it)

Save Pasta Water:
When draining pasta many people and tip away all of the pasta water. Don't do this, always keep at least one cup of pasta water on the side. When you mix your pasta with a sauce, adding some additional pasta water helps combine the ingredients and makes the pasta creamy. Dishes such as carbonara require the use of pasta water.

Quality Ingredients:
Italian cuisine often relies on simple, fresh ingredients, so use the best quality produce, meats, cheeses, and olive oil you can find. Fresh herbs and vegetables can make a huge difference in flavour.

Respect Seasonality:
Italian cooking is deeply rooted in the seasons, so try to use ingredients that are in season for the freshest and most flavourful dishes. Seasonal produce will also be more affordable and environmentally friendly.

Learn Proper Techniques:
Take the time to learn basic Italian cooking techniques such as properly sautéing garlic, making a good tomato sauce from scratch, and cooking pasta al dente. These fundamental skills will serve as the foundation for many Italian dishes.

Don't Overcomplicate:
Italian cuisine is known for its simplicity, so don't feel the need to overcomplicate recipes with too many ingredients or elaborate techniques. Let the flavours of the ingredients shine through with minimal fuss.

Balance Flavours:
Italian dishes often balance sweet, salty, sour, and bitter flavours, so pay attention to achieving the right balance in your dishes. For example, a splash of balsamic vinegar can add a touch of acidity to balance the richness of a tomato sauce.

Use Fresh Herbs:
Fresh herbs like basil, parsley, and oregano are essential in Italian cooking and can add brightness and depth of flavour to your dishes. If possible, use fresh herbs instead of dried for the best results.

Cook Pasta Properly:
Cook pasta al dente, which means it should be cooked until it's firm to the bite. This ensures that the pasta maintains its texture and doesn't become mushy when combined with sauces.

Experiment with Regional Cuisine:
Italy's regional cuisines vary widely, so don't be afraid to explore dishes from different regions. Try your hand at making risotto from the north, pasta dishes from central Italy, and seafood dishes from the south to discover the diverse flavours of Italian cuisine.

Finish with Extra Virgin Olive Oil:
A drizzle of high-quality extra virgin olive oil can elevate the flavours of many Italian dishes, so always keep a bottle on hand for finishing touches.

Enjoy with Wine:
Italian food is often enjoyed with a glass of Italian wine! Pair your dishes with a complementary wine from the same region for an authentic dining experience.

Use Extra Virgin Olive Oil
You can use the cheaper olive oil, but if you can use extra virgin olive oil. My favourite is cold pressed, but it's quite expensive. Shop around and try different kinds.

Don't Burn the Garlic!
When garlic burns it turns bitter and taste gross. It can actually ruin your meal. Don't throw garlic into very hot oil for too long. If you're cooking a base for your dish, eg; frying some onion, celery and meat, add the garlic last and stir it in. Also to help prevent the garlic from bring in the hot oil add a splash of water.

Re-pot Basil Plants:

When you buy potted basil from the super market, transfer it to a bigger pot and use high quality nutritious soil. The basil plant will flourish so long as it gets sunlight every day and you make sure the soil doesn't dry out. In the winter keep it inside at the window. Whenever it starts to look unhealthy transfer it to a bigger pot along with some fresh soil. You can also take cuttings from thinner stems and place them in water, new roots will grow from the stem and you can start growing more plants. Unlimited basil all year round from one single plant!

We hope you enjoyed our recipe book!

Printed in Great Britain
by Amazon

c4683d0c-e982-4d7c-be21-c2933d5b8f1dR01